REVIVING CAREERS

SUCCESS WHEN RE-ENTERING THE WORKFORCE

- ☑ SEARCHING
- ☑ POSITIONING
- ☑ NETWORKING
- ☑ CAMPAIGNING
- ☑ INTERVIEWING
- ☑ TRANSITIONING

Reviving Careers: Success for Women Re-Entering the Workforce
Copyright © 2018 by Julie Visser. All rights reserved.

Published by JA Talent Partners, LLC, Encinitas, CA
978-1-7327826-0-0 (Paperback)

All trademarks are the property of their respective owners.

This book is intended to provide accurate information with regards to its subject matter. However, in times of rapid change, ensuring all information provided is entirely accurate and up-to-date at all times is not always possible. Therefore, the author and publisher accept no responsibility for inaccuracies or omissions and specifically disclaim any liability, loss or risk, personal, professional or otherwise, which may be incurred as a consequence, directly or indirectly, of the use and/ or application of any of the contents of this book.

Without limiting the rights under copyright reserved above, no part of this publication may be reproduced, stored in or introduced into a retrieval system, or transmitted in any form or by any means (electronic, mechanical , photocopying, recording or otherwise), without the prior written permission of both the copyright owner and the above publisher of this book, except by a reviewer who wishes to quote brief passages in connection with a review written for insertion in a magazine, newspaper, broadcast, website, blog or other outlet.

Publishing Consultant: David Wogahn, DavidWogahn.com

REVIVING CAREERS

TABLE OF CONTENTS

PHASE ONE: JOB SEARCH OBJECTIVE
- Job Search Objective 2
- Self-Evaluation Perspective 3–4
- Career Self-Assessment 5–8
- Career Base Scoring 9
- Personal Characteristics 10
- Skills Inventory 11
- Value Triggers 12
- Strength Triggers 13
- Professional Objective Summary 14
- Career Options Matrix 15

PHASE TWO: POSITIONING YOURSELF IN THE MARKETPLACE
- Positioning Yourself in the Marketplace 18
- Identifying Accomplishments Worksheet 19
- Success Story Worksheet 20–21
- Gap Positioning Statement 22
- Preparing Your Gap Positioning Statement 23
- Professional Positioning Statement 24
- Sample Professional Positioning Statement 25
- Resume Essentials 26
- Resume Critique Checklist 27
- Chronological Resume 28
- Functional Resume 29
- Writing Cover Letters 30
- Gap Situation Letter Examples 31
- LinkedIn Profile 32–34

PHASE THREE: NETWORKING EFFECTIVELY
- What Is Networking and Why Network? 36
- Map Your Contact Network 37–38
- How to Approach Network Meetings 39
- LinkedIn Tips for Your Job Search 40–41
- Types of Recruiters 42

REVIVING CAREERS

   10 Things to Know About Working with Recruiters 43
   6 Tips When Communicating with Hiring Managers 44

PHASE FOUR: JOB SEARCH CAMPAIGNING

   Job Search Campaigns 46–47
   Create Objectives and Choose Tactics 48
   Target Jobs and Companies Worksheet 49
   Target Markets and Companies 50
   Target Company Worksheets 51–52
   Search Methods 53
   10 Best Sources of Jobs 54–55
   Finding Jobs Online Today 56

PHASE FIVE: INTERVIEWING AND JOB OFFERS

   Types of Interviews 58–60
   Company Research 61
   Securing the Interview 62–63
   Steps in Preparing for an Interview 64
   10 Tips for Interview Day 65
   Asking the Right Questions 66
   Questions to Prepare for When Re-Entering the Workforce 67
   Traditional vs. Behavioral-Based Interviews 68
   Cultivating and Negotiating Job Offers 69
   Negotiating Your Salary and Setting Expectations 70

PHASE SIX: TRANSITIONING INTO THE WORKFORCE

   Transition into the Workplace 72
   Technology in the Workplace 73
   Long-Term Career Planning 74

JOB SEARCH OBJECTIVE

PHASE ONE

OBJECTIVE

JOB SEARCH OBJECTIVE

Every successful program begins with setting objectives and in a job search, the objective is to find a meaningful career opportunity. When contacting your network or interviewing, you need to clearly communicate exactly what type of position you desire and why you would be the best candidate for the role.

Conducting a thorough self-assessment will guide you in creating a professional objective that is concise. This objective will be unique and will distinctly convey the career path you are seeking. Assessing your skills, competencies, values, strengths, personal characteristics, interests and motivation will allow you to define and communicate the kind of work you will be most satisfied performing.

Your job search objective will set the direction for your marketing strategy and will be reflective of your resume and LinkedIn profile. This will let others know you are focused, aware of your professional aspirations and understand the value you can provide to an organization.

Having a focused objective will lead to a targeted, effective and rapid job search, allowing you to communicate with confidence and consistency. Without a defined objective, time and energy is wasted.

OBJECTIVE

SELF-EVALUATION PERSPECTIVE

Please complete each phrase to make a complete sentence to reflect your beliefs, intuitions and feelings about reentering the workforce.

1. Currently, I believe _____

2. What I would like most from a career is _____

3. If possible, the next stage of my career would be _____

4. People tell me I should _____

5. One day I aspire to _____

6. If I could do anything I would _____

   because _____

7. Others see me as _____

8. I am at my best when _____

9. I would like a career which would give me an opportunity to _____

10. I consider myself _____

OBJECTIVE

SELF-EVALUATION PERSPECTIVE

11. Others compliment me on _____
    _____

12. I should attempt to _____
    _____

13. I see my strengths as _____
    _____

14. The type of work I am most interested in is _____
    _____

    because _____
    _____

15. If I receive advice for anything, it's likely to be _____
    _____

16. I could be a more effective employee if _____
    _____

17. My greatest sense of achievement comes from _____
    _____

18. I believe I am at my best when _____
    _____

19. I am most satisfied when _____
    _____

20. I would like to re-enter the workforce, so I can _____
    _____

Thoughtfully consider your answers as this will allow you to be self-aware when creating your personal job search objective.

OBJECTIVE

CAREER SELF-ASSESSMENT

Please rate each statement with the number which best reflects how you feel.

Strongly Disagree	Disagree	Agree	Strongly Agree
1	2	3	4

_____ 1. I want to become an expert at what I do so others will seek my advice.

_____ 2. I am most satisfied with my work when I integrate the efforts of others toward a common goal.

_____ 3. My ultimate goal is to have a career that will allow me the flexibility to work my own way and on my own schedule.

_____ 4. Job security and stability are more important to me than flexibility and autonomy.

_____ 5. I am always searching for ideas that would allow me to start my own business.

_____ 6. I will feel acknowledged in my job only if I have a sense of having made a real contribution to society.

_____ 7. I imagine a career where I will always have challenging problems to solve.

_____ 8. I would rather leave my company than have a job that does not allow me the flexibility to care for personal or family needs as they arise.

_____ 9. I will feel accomplished in my career only if I continue to improve on my skills and competencies.

_____ 10. I would like to be the leader of an entire organization.

_____ 11. I am most happy when working in an environment that allows me complete freedom to define my own tasks and schedules.

_____ 12. I would not stay at a company that would ask me to do work that would endanger my job security.

OBJECTIVE

CAREER SELF-ASSESSMENT

Please rate each statement with the number which best reflects how you feel.

Strongly Disagree	Disagree	Agree	Strongly Agree
1	2	3	4

_____ 13. Constructing my own business is more interesting to me than being an executive in a public or private company.

_____ 14. I feel most gratified when I utilize my talents to assist others.

_____ 15. I will feel acknowledged in my career only if I continuously conquer difficult challenges.

_____ 16. My perfect career will allow me a true work/life balance.

_____ 17. I would prefer being an expert in my field over holding a general manager position.

_____ 18. I will only feel successful if I become an important executive within a corporation.

_____ 19. I will be happy with my position only if I manage to have complete autonomy and freedom when defining my work.

_____ 20. I look for opportunities that will give me a sense of stability and security.

_____ 21. Creating something that is the result of my own skill and effort is what provides me fulfillment.

_____ 22. Utilizing my skills and talents to make the world a better place is what drives my career decisions.

_____ 23. I have been most fulfilled in my career when I have been challenged with problems and have been able to resolve tough issues.

_____ 24. I only feel accomplished when I have been able to balance my personal, family and work needs.

OBJECTIVE

CAREER SELF-ASSESSMENT

Please rate each statement with the number which best reflects how you feel.

Strongly Disagree	Disagree	Agree	Strongly Agree
1	2	3	4

_____ 25. I dream of a career that will allow me to feel a sense of stability.

_____ 26. I will feel accomplished in my career only if I have developed a business based on my ideas.

_____ 27. General management is more appealing to me than managing a specific area of expertise.

_____ 28. I aspire to have a career that will give me a sense of safety and security.

_____ 29. I aspire to have a career that truly contributes to society.

_____ 30. Balancing the needs of my personal and professional life is more important to me than an executive position.

_____ 31. The opportunity to complete an assignment on my own, free of restrictions, is very important to me.

_____ 32. I would rather leave my company than accept a new role that would take me away from my area of expertise.

_____ 33. I would rather leave my company than accept a new role that would weaken my ability to help others.

_____ 34. I find the most gratification in my work when I have been able to use my expertise to move a big project forward.

_____ 35. It is important to me at this stage in my life to have a sense of complete financial security.

OBJECTIVE

CAREER SELF-ASSESSMENT

Please rate each statement with the number which best reflects how you feel.

Strongly Disagree	Disagree	Agree	Strongly Agree
1	2	3	4

_____ 36. I would prefer to leave my company rather than accept a position that would remove me from the direction of general management.

_____ 37. I prefer career opportunities that strongly challenge my problem-solving and competitive skills.

_____ 38. I aspire to start my own business one day.

_____ 39. I have always searched for career opportunities that reduce disruption with my personal life.

_____ 40. I would rather leave my company than accept a new position that would decrease my independence.

Now please go back over all of the items and choose the five that are most undeniably how you feel. Circle those numbers and give each of those statements an additional five points on the scoring sheet.

OBJECTIVE

CAREER BASE SCORING

SCORING INSTRUCTIONS: Transfer your ratings for each item to the scoring table below, being sure to put the correct number of points for each item next to that item's number.

TF	GM	AU	SE	EN	SV	CH	LS
1. _____	2. _____	3. _____	4. _____	5. _____	6. _____	7. _____	8. _____
9. _____	10. _____	11. _____	12. _____	13. _____	14. _____	15. _____	16. _____
17. _____	18. _____	19. _____	20. _____	21. _____	22. _____	23. _____	24. _____
25. _____	26. _____	27. _____	28. _____	29. _____	30. _____	31. _____	32. _____
33. _____	34. _____	35. _____	36. _____	37. _____	38. _____	39. _____	40. _____
Total _____	Total _____	Total _____	Total _____	Total _____	Total _____	Total _____	Total _____

Add the numbers in each column. The higher the number, the more that career base represents your preferences.

- TF   TECHNICAL FUNCTION
- GM GENERAL MANAGEMENT
- AU AUTONOMY
- SE   SECURITY
- EN ENTREPRENEURIAL
- SV SERVICE
- CH CHALLENGE
- LS   LIFESTYLE

OBJECTIVE

PERSONAL CHARACTERISTICS

Review the list below and select the eight traits that you feel best describe you. Of these eight that you checked, circle the three that you feel are most accurate. You will use these in your positioning statement.

- ❏ Accurate
- ❏ Adventurous
- ❏ Artistic
- ❏ Assertive
- ❏ Challenging
- ❏ Committed
- ❏ Communicative
- ❏ Compassionate
- ❏ Confident
- ❏ Creative
- ❏ Curious
- ❏ Dedicated
- ❏ Dependable
- ❏ Diligent
- ❏ Efficient
- ❏ Emotional
- ❏ Energetic
- ❏ Entertaining
- ❏ Enthusiastic
- ❏ Expressive
- ❏ Humorous
- ❏ Imaginative
- ❏ Independent
- ❏ Inquisitive
- ❏ Intelligent
- ❏ Kind
- ❏ Leader
- ❏ Levelheaded
- ❏ Loyal
- ❏ Original
- ❏ People-oriented
- ❏ Perfectionist
- ❏ Personable
- ❏ Persuasive
- ❏ Positive attitude
- ❏ Practical
- ❏ Productive
- ❏ Rational
- ❏ Responsible
- ❏ Responsive
- ❏ Self-assured
- ❏ Self-controlled
- ❏ Self-starter
- ❏ Sensitive
- ❏ Sociable
- ❏ Stable
- ❏ Tolerant
- ❏ Trustworthy
- ❏ Takes initiative
- ❏ Other _____

OBJECTIVE

SKILLS INVENTORY

Select three skills that best describe your experience, education and achievements.

COMMUNICATING
Corresponding
Editing
Interviewing
Managing conflict
Negotiating
Public speaking
Writing
Drawing
Facilitating
Mediating
Presenting
Relating to customers

COORDINATING
Following up
Scheduling
Correcting
Reporting

DEVELOPING PEOPLE
Assessing performance
Counseling
Helping others
Teaching
Training
Coaching
Motivating
Team building

FINANCIAL MANAGEMENT
Auditing
Financial analysis
Fundraising
Budgeting
Cost accounting
Financial planning

DATA MANAGEMENT
Analyzing data
Research
Inventory
Assessing data
Assessing quality
Measuring
Setting standards

MANAGING PEOPLE
Approving
Developing procedures
Directing
Implementing
Creating policy
Managing people
Managing tasks
Delegating
Developing systems
Instructing
Making decisions
Managing projects

ORGANIZING
Administering
Projecting
Setting priorities
Restructuring

PLANNING
Analyzing
Designing
Developing strategy
Conceptualizing
Developing policy

SELLING / MARKETING
Advertising
Sales management
Pricing
Relating to clients
Proposals
Analyzing markets
Marketing
Promoting
Selling

SERVING
Client relations
Communication
Handling complaints

TECHNICAL SKILLS
Computer
Systems
Engineering
Programming
Designing
Developing
Inventing
Manufacturing

OTHER SKILLS
_____
_____
_____
_____
_____
_____

OBJECTIVE

VALUE TRIGGERS

Values guide our actions so the goal here is to determine what really matters to you and align values and actions. Draw a line through those that are less important to you and circle and rank the three words that are most important.

Accomplishment	Cooperation	Innovation	Recognition
Accountability	Courage	Integrity	Reliability
Achievement	Creativity	Intelligence	Respect
Adaptability	Curiosity	Joy	Responsibility
Advancement	Determination	Knowledge	Results
Adventure	Diversity	Learning	Risk
Affection	Equality	Leisure	Security
Altruism	Excitement	Loyalty	Service
Balance	Faith	Mastery	Simplicity
Beauty	Family	Openness	Solitude
Belonging	Freedom	Order	Spirituality
Challenge	Fun	Originality	Spontaneity
Clarity	Growth	Passion	Stability
Commitment	Harmony	Patience	Structure
Community	Health	Play	Tradition
Compassion	Honesty	Power	Tranquility
Connection	Impact	Prestige	Variety
Contribution	Independence	Productivity	Wealth
Control	Influence	Quality	Wisdom

VALUES NOT LISTED:

_____

_____

OBJECTIVE

STRENGTH TRIGGERS

Circle all the strengths you can be counted on to consistently deliver. Place a "+" next to those circled strengths that really energize you and a "-" next to those that leave you feeling drained or depleted (e.g. being responsible is a strength of mine, but it depletes me.) Choose your top three strengths that you really enjoy using and these will be employed in your positioning statement.

Accountable	Decisive	Kind	Realistic
Adaptable	Determined	Knowledgeable	Receptive
Adventurous	Direct	Loyal	Reliable
Affectionate	Disciplined	Mature	Reserved
Altruistic	Driven	Observant	Resilient
Analytical	Easygoing	Open	Resourceful
Appreciative	Empathetic	Organized	Respectful
Approachable	Energetic	Original	Responsible
Caring	Enterprising	Passionate	Self-assured
Challenging	Focused	Patient	Self-controlled
Clear	Generous	Persuasive	Sensible
Committed	Harmonious	Playful	Spontaneous
Compassionate	Honest	Positive	Strategic
Competent	Imaginative	Powerful	Supportive
Connected	Inclusive	Practical	Tactful
Consistent	Independent	Precise	Thoughtful
Cooperative	Influential	Protective	Visionary
Creative	Inspiring	Purposeful	Warm
Curious	Integrity	Quick	Wise

STRENGTHS NOT LISTED:

_____

_____

_____

OBJECTIVE

PROFESSIONAL OBJECTIVE SUMMARY

Your self-assessment material should be consistent with your professional objective. Use this as an outline to create your professional objective.

CAREER VISION / PREFERENCE

_____
_____
_____
_____
_____

PERSONAL CHARACTERISTICS (PG. 10)
1. _____
2. _____
3. _____
4. _____

SKILLS (PG. 11)
1. _____
2. _____
3. _____
4. _____

VALUES (PG. 12)
1. _____
2. _____
3. _____
4. _____

STRENGTHS (PG. 13)
1. _____
2. _____
3. _____
4. _____

PROFESSIONAL OBJECTIVE STATEMENT (WILL BE UTILIZED ON RESUME)
A PROFESSIONAL OBJECTIVE is a short, targeted statement that clearly outlines your career direction while simultaneously positioning you as someone who meets the needs of the employer. Your objective is carefully researched and tailored to fit the job you're applying for. [Example: To leverage my ten years of client-facing experience, public speaking skills, and expertise in the human resource industry in a public relations role with JA Talent Partners.]

_____
_____
_____
_____

OBJECTIVE

CAREER OPTIONS MATRIX

Career Option	Why I Would Like This	Strengths to Leverage	Benefits	Costs

POSITIONING YOURSELF IN THE MARKETPLACE

PHASE TWO

POSITIONING

POSITIONING YOURSELF IN THE MARKETPLACE

In today's job hunting environment, the most successful job seekers are those who understand the value of marketing and apply to themselves those principles that companies have used for years to successfully sell their products.

When re-entering the workforce, you are the product. You should examine what characteristics, features and skills make you unique. These features can include work experience, leadership experience, professional relationships, volunteer work, education and training.

What is the one thing that makes you different than any other job seeker applying for the same job? What are your accomplishments (not duties or job titles)? How attractive a product are you? What will make you more attractive to employers? How do you communicate your gap in employment? How do you package yourself through your cover letter, resume and LinkedIn profile? Are you able to state your positioning statement in 15 words or less?

Creating a positioning statement will help you better understand yourself as a product/brand and will give you the confidence to get the job you really want and deserve.

POSITIONING

IDENTIFYING ACCOMPLISHMENTS WORKSHEET

Review the questions and place a check next to those that apply to you. Note the accomplishment and the skills used to achieve it.

❏ Did you identify a problem and solve it? What were the results?
_____

❏ Did you introduce a new system or procedure that made work easier or more accurate?
_____

❏ Have you saved an organization time or money? How much? What positive impact did the savings have on this organization (company, charity, school)?
_____

❏ Did you increase productivity or reduce downtime? By how much? How did the savings affect the bottom line?
_____

❏ Did you effectively manage systems or people? What were the results of your efforts?
_____

❏ Did you participate in decision making or planning? What contributions did you make? What were the results of your efforts?
_____

❏ Did you write any major reports, programs, publications or newsletters?
_____

❏ Did you improve the efficiency of people or operations? What were the results?
_____

❏ Were you involved in a start-up or shut-down? What were the challenges you faced?
_____

❏ Were you a liaison between people? How were you able to make things run more efficiently?
_____

POSITIONING

SUCCESS STORY WORKSHEET

In this exercise, you will analyze your most important work/school/life-related achievements. Fill in the skills or personal characteristics you used in each accomplishment.

You should have a minimum of five success stories prior to an interview

SITUATION

- ➢ Describe the situation
- ➢ Explain why this situation was causing a problem
- ➢ Be clear and concise with relative information

DIFFICULTIES

- ➢ Describe the obstacles you faced
- ➢ Do not put blame on others
- ➢ Remain positive when discussing difficulties

PERFORMANCE

- ➢ List the actions you took
- ➢ Describe why you took these specific actions
- ➢ Give credit to those who helped you achieve results

RESULTS/ACCOMPLISHMENTS

- ➢ Describe the results you helped obtain
- ➢ Be specific with the outcome and results
- ➢ Discuss what you and others learned from the situation

POSITIONING

SUCCESS STORY WORKSHEET

SITUATION	DIFFICULTIES
Describe the situation	**Describe the obstacles you faced**

PERFORMANCE	RESULTS/ACCOMPLISHMENTS
List the actions you took	**Describe the results you helped obtain**
Skills Used:	

POSITIONING

GAP POSITIONING STATEMENT

BE HONEST

Whatever the reason for your time away from work, honesty is always the best policy. During the entire process of your job search, maintain your integrity and demonstrate it. This being said, your answers should be well-thought-out and polished.

BE PREPARED

Stumbling your way through your first sit-down interview is as unimpressive as showing up late. Just as you would prep to discuss your previous positions, employers are going to ask about your time off, so be ready to address this. Many people have taken time off to raise children, care for a sick parent or travel the world. Employers understand that life happens.

Once you have identified your accomplishments, create a short, compelling statement to use in interviews. Think of this as your press release because it is the communication that tells the world about your transition. An effective gap/transition statement is brief, positive and non-defensive. It lets others know that exiting and re-entering the workforce is your choice. This is your opportunity to make an impact and set yourself apart from other applicants.

BE CONFIDENT

While the thought of discussing your gap in employment might make you feel uneasy, don't panic. Resume gaps are not as uncommon as many people may think. Being prepared for whatever comes your way and having confidence in the skills you've attained during a break go a long way to bridging the gap.

BE POSITIVE

Make sure you emphasize any constructive activities during your gap period such as volunteer work, continued education, consulting or freelance work. Finally, exude enthusiasm for returning to work and make a very strong case for why you would be an excellent fit for your target company. Your gap in employment can make you an even stronger candidate for the position.

POSITIONING

PREPARING YOUR GAP POSITIONING STATEMENT

Write a carefully constructed statement that explains why you are in the market for a new position and practice it out loud.

SAMPLE GAP POSITIONING STATEMENTS

"As a result of my children being grown, I have made a conscious decision to re-enter the workforce. I am looking for an opportunity that will take full advantage of my ability to make an impact on how organizations acquire top talent."

"The recent change in my life has afforded me the opportunity to explore new options. With my record of financial planning, problem solving and fundraising accomplishments, my objective is to locate a position as a Project Manager for a non-profit organization."

"After focusing on a new mentoring program for inner city youth, I would like to transfer my interpersonal and problem-solving skills to the professional workforce. I am seeking a position with a company focused on the youth population."

YOUR GAP POSITION STATEMENT

_____

_____

_____

_____

POSITIONING

PROFESSIONAL POSITIONING STATEMENT

Your professional positioning statement should be under two minutes. Your statement should be structured around the four following categories:

1. **PROFESSION**
   Begin by stating your professional identity in the present tense. For example, "I am a recent college graduate with a BA degree in Human Resources"

2. **EXPERTISE**
   When expressing your expertise, focus on the competencies and skills you have identified. For example, "I am a recent college graduate with a degree in human resources and have internship experience in talent acquisition"

3. **TYPES OF ORGANIZATIONS**
   Summarize the environment or organizations in which you have worked/interned, such as a Fortune 100 firm, small consulting firm or non-profit entity. You may mention other types of activities, such as teaching, participating on a school board, or holding leadership roles.

4. **UNIQUE STRENGTHS**
   Articulate the qualities that differentiate you from others in your field. While remaining humble, do share why you believe you are qualified for the role and why you would be a good match for the company.

Different methods can be used to introduce strengths and expertise, but your Professional Positioning Statement should create a clear impression of your value to potential employers.

POSITIONING

SAMPLE PROFESSIONAL POSITIONING STATEMENT

"I am a human resource professional with an expertise in talent acquisition. My strengths include communication, coaching and relating to internal clients. For example, in my last role I tripled the size of the talent acquisition function, while streamlining hiring efficiencies, and improving the quality of hires. I have worked with fast-growing start-up organizations as well as Fortune 100 companies."

"I am an information systems specialist focusing on technology for education institutions. My field of expertise is diverse. I have worked with small private schools, as well as large public school districts. My strengths include data administration, strategic planning, data warehousing, development and implementation."

YOUR PROFESSIONAL POSITIONING STATEMENT

_____

_____

_____

_____

POSITIONING

RESUME ESSENTIALS

Chronological Resume vs. Functional Resume

CHRONOLOGICAL RESUME

The **Chronological Resume** is the most frequently used and accepted resume format when:

- ✓ Your career history shows growth and development
- ✓ Your job objective is similar to your recent experience
- ✓ Your previous employers are well known
- ✓ You are applying for a position in traditional fields or organizations

FUNCTIONAL RESUME

The **Functional Resume** is designed to stress the qualifications of the job seeker, with less emphasis on specific employers and dates. The functional resume is helpful when:

- ✓ Your objective is very different from your experience
- ✓ You want to emphasize skills/abilities not used in recent work experience
- ✓ Your experience has been gained in different unrelated jobs
- ✓ **You are entering the job market after an absence**

TEN PARTS OF A RESUME

1. Heading
2. Professional Objective (Optional and Targeted)
3. Summary Statement
4. Employment History
5. Responsibilities Statements
6. Accomplishment Statements
7. Education
8. Professional Development, Training, Software Proficiencies
9. Memberships
10. Other—Languages, Licenses, Certificates, Military Experience, Publications

POSITIONING

RESUME CRITIQUE CHECKLIST

Resumes get less than a 15-second glance at the first screening. Be sure you can answer yes to the following:

FIRST IMPRESSION:
- ❏ Does the resume look original and not based on a template?
- ❏ Is the resume inviting to read, with clear sections and ample white space?
- ❏ Does the design look professional rather than like a simple typing job?
- ❏ Is a qualifications summary included so the reader immediately knows your value proposition?
- ❏ Is the resume's length appropriate (1-2 pages)?
- ❏ Is the font appropriate for the career level and industry?
- ❏ Is the font size and spacing consistent throughout the resume?
- ❏ Is the work history listed in reverse chronological order (most recent job first)?

CAREER GOAL
- ❏ Is the career objective included toward the top of the resume in a headline, objective or qualifications summary?
- ❏ Is the resume targeted to a specific career goal rather than trying to be a one-size-fits-all document? Does the career goal match the job you are applying for?
- ❏ Is the current objective clearly stated?

ACCOMPLISHMENTS
- ❏ Does your resume include a solid listing of career/school accomplishments?
- ❏ Are the accomplishments quantified by using numbers, percentages, dollar amounts or other concrete measures of success?
- ❏ Do accomplishment statements begin with strong, varied action verbs?
- ❏ Are accomplishments separated from responsibilities?

RELEVANCE
- ❏ Is the information relevant to the hiring manager's needs?
- ❏ Does your resume content support the career goal?
- ❏ Is the resume keyword-rich, packed with appropriate buzzwords and industry acronyms?

WRITING STYLE
- ❏ Is the resume written in an implied first-person voice with personal pronouns (such as "I" and "my") avoided?
- ❏ Is the content flow logical and easy to understand?
- ❏ Is the resume error free, with no careless typos, grammar, or syntax mistakes? Have someone you trust proofread your resume.

POSITIONING

CHRONOLOGICAL RESUME OUTLINE

Name
Address | Phone
Email | LinkedIn Address

Professional Objective
(Target to a specific job opportunity)

POSITIONING STATEMENT

PROFESSIONAL EXPERIENCE

Company, City, State (most recent job)
Title
Key responsibilities
- XXX
- XXX

Accomplishments
- XXX
- XXX

Company, City, State
Title
Key responsibilities
- XXX
- XXX

Accomplishments
- XXX
- XXX

EDUCATION
Degree | Major | School

SKILLS
- XXX
- XXX

INTERESTS | ATTRIBUTES (OPTIONAL)
- XXX
- XXX

POSITIONING

FUNCTIONAL RESUME OUTLINE

Utilize functional format if you do not have a paid employment history

Name
Address | Phone
Email | LinkedIn Address

Professional Objective
(Target to a specific job opportunity)

POSITIONING STATEMENT

SKILLS SUMMARY
- XXX
- XXX
- XXX

PROFESSIONAL EXPERIENCE
Include responsibilities and accomplishments from paid and unpaid experiences
- XXX
- XXX
- XXX

WORK HISTORY (PAID OR UNPAID)

Company, City, State
Title **Dates**

Company, City, State
Title **Dates**

EDUCATION
Degree | Major | School

POSITIONING

WRITING COVER LETTERS

Cover Letter Format

Date
Address
Salutation

PARAGRAPH ONE

Explain why you are applying for this opportunity in a way that arouses interest. Display your knowledge of the person and/or the company.

PARAGRAPH TWO

Briefly describe your qualifications and accomplishments and relate these to the specific job opening.

PARAGRAPH THREE

Answer the question: Why should the company hire you?

PARAGRAPH FOUR

Take the initiative, request action, ask for an interview, suggest a time to meet and tell the employer when you will follow up.

If the company requests that you do not call the recruiter, find another contact in the organization you can reach out to. The key is to gain access to an inside track within the department or company.

POSITIONING

GAP SITUATION LETTER EXAMPLES

MEDICAL LEAVE

After taking time off to undergo back surgery, I left XXX Co. on excellent terms to focus on my recovery. As I regained my strength, I went to school part-time and received certifications in _____ and _____. Now fully recovered, I have been given an "excellent" bill of health by my doctor and am highly motivated to return to the full-time workforce.

TIME OFF CARING FOR AN ILL FAMILY MEMBER

For the last two years, I served as primary caregiver to my father, who had been diagnosed with a terminal illness. During this difficult period, I kept my work skills updated by independently studying _____ and actively participating in industry news groups. At this time, I am available to return to work, and am confident that I would be an asset to your team.

TIME OFF RAISING CHILDREN

After stepping away from the workforce to start a family, I am eager to resume my professional career now that my children are school-aged. I have kept my skills and connections current through active volunteer work, including leadership roles in school and charitable organizations.

CAREER CHANGE

Though successful in my _____ career, I have realized that the aspects of my work that I find the most rewarding are all in _____-related functions. I am currently pursuing a full-time position in this area and am confident in my ability to excel in this field.

TEMP EXPERIENCE

Most recently, I have contracted with XXX Agency and have completed a number of interesting assignments (detailed on the attached resume). While this work is rewarding, the short-term nature of temping does not provide the kind of enduring, value-added contributions I find to be most fulfilling. I am currently pursuing a full-time role in _____.

POSITIONING

LinkedIn PROFILE

LinkedIn is the largest professional networking tool online. For individuals in career transition, an updated LinkedIn profile is very important. This site is the single most important social networking tool for your career.

These days it takes more than a resume to stand out in a competitive job market. A profile that grabs attention on LinkedIn could make a difference as well.

HOW TO SET UP YOUR LinkedIn PROFILE — KEEP IT PROFESSIONAL

SIGN UP AT LinkedIn.COM
Take time to make your profile 100% complete. The more complete your profile, the better the odds that recruiters will find you. LinkedIn will measure the "completeness" of your profile, which you can view on your profile page.

GET A CUSTOM URL
It is much easier to publicize your profile with a customized URL (linkedin.yourname) How to do this? On the Edit Profile screen, at the bottom of the gray window that shows your basic information, you'll see a Public Profile URL. Click "Edit" next to the URL and specify what you'd like your address to be. When you're finished, click Set Custom URL.

UPLOAD A RECENT, CLEAR, PROFESSIONAL PHOTO
Your profile is 11 times more likely to be viewed if you add a picture, so choose your photo wisely and ensure it is appropriate for your career field.

WRITE A HEADLINE AS YOUR VALUE PROPOSITION
Use this space to showcase your specialty and/or value proposition. The more specific you can be about what sets you apart from the competition the better.

POSITIONING

LinkedIn PROFILE

USE TARGET WORDS AND PHRASES

View the job descriptions of the positions you are interested in applying for. Use key words and phrases and ensure they are sprinkled throughout your summary and experience. These are the words recruiters are searching for when they are looking for potential employees.

SUMMARY SPACE

Your summary should be 3-5 paragraphs long, preferably with a bulleted section in the middle. It should address your work passions, key skills, unique qualifications and a list of industries you've had exposure to over the years. Don't be shy, highlight your accomplishments with facts and figures. Be warm and invite interaction. Inject your personality, let people know your values and what you do outside of work. You want people to want to know you.

AVOID OVERUSED BUZZWORDS

Be original—don't use responsible, creative, effective, analytical, strategic, patient, expert, organizational, driven and innovative. These are the most overused buzzwords on LinkedIn. These may be your base strength/value triggers, but find synonyms to expand your vocabulary.

TREAT YOUR PROFILE LIKE YOUR RESUME

Make sure your experience section has bullet points that describe what you did, how well you did it and whom it impacted. The difference between your resume and LinkedIn profile is that using first person on LinkedIn is acceptable: "I am a passionate recruiter who hired over 100 new people last year" instead of "Sara Brown is a passionate recruiter."

INCLUDE A CURRENT JOB ENTRY, EVEN WHEN YOU ARE UNEMPLOYED

If you only list the past positions you have held in the experience section but show nothing current, your profile will most likely be overlooked in most searches. Why? Because most recruiters exclusively use the current title box to search for candidates. If you are unemployed, create a dummy job listing in the current section that includes the job title(s) you are targeting—"Entering the workforce/financial analyst"—followed by a phrase like "In transition" or "Seeking new opportunity" in the company name box.

POSITIONING

LinkedIn PROFILE

JOIN GROUPS

LinkedIn groups are an incredible resource and they can do wonders for your job search. By joining groups associated with your profession or industry, you will show that you're engaged in your field. But more importantly, you'll instantly be connected to people and part of relevant discussions in your field.

HAVE AT LEAST 100 CONNECTIONS

Having 100 or fewer connections on LinkedIn tells recruiters one of three things: 1. You are a recluse who knows few people, 2. You are paranoid about connecting with others, 3. Technology and social media scare you. None of these conclusions are good, so have at least 100 connections as a starting point.

Upload your address book, but do not add random people. LinkedIn can shut down your account if enough people reject your request, stating they do not know you. When asking to connect with someone, use "we've done business together" rather than "friend".

MAKE SURE PEOPLE CAN FIND YOU

Include your email address, blog, Twitter handle or any other social media sites in the contact information section of your resume.

EXUDE ENTHUSIASM

The people who get hired are those that are excited about what they do. Join and participate in groups related to your field. Use your status line to relate things you are doing within your field. Share interesting articles or news. Connect with leaders in your industry to network and share information.

BE CONSISTENT

Log on to LinkedIn every day as consistency shows you are an active participant on this business networking site.

SHOWCASE VOLUNTEER EXPERIENCE, ORGANIZATIONS AND CAUSES YOU CARE ABOUT

Many hiring managers view volunteer experience equal to formal work experience, particularly if you are entering the workforce after an interruption.

NETWORKING EFFECTIVELY

PHASE THREE

NETWORKING

WHAT IS NETWORKING?

Networking is simply talking to others, either formally or informally, about your job search and career goals. Networking is not "asking" for a job, it is giving and receiving information, ideas, referrals, recommendations, leads and support with others. Networking is how you convert 10 great contacts into 75-100 connections.

WHY NETWORK?

Many available jobs are never advertised online, instead, recruiters and managers rely on networking referrals to find and attract potential job candidates.

The old saying, "It's not what you know, it's who you know" is still true in today's business environment.

- Fewer than 20% of jobs are filled by someone responding to a job posting
- Approximately 45% of jobs are filled by networking efforts per LinkedIn

WHAT TO REMEMBER?

- Be ready to network anytime, anyplace and with anyone
- Let people know you are in the job market, you never know who is listening
- Don't be afraid to ask for a networking meeting, as face-to-face time is valuable. Be considerate of others' time and come prepared with questions and a well-thought-out objective for the meeting.

NETWORKING

MAP YOUR CONTACT NETWORK

Write the names of people from your life—this is the beginning of your network!

Friends/Relatives/Neighbors	Past Coworkers & Colleagues	Past Clients, Customers and Business Associates

Spouse's/Partner's Network	Alumni of Your School/ Teachers/Professors	Children's Network

Reach out to each individual to let them know you are seeking to enter the workforce. Communicate your professional objective and ask for referrals, a conversation or an in-person meeting.

NETWORKING

MAP YOUR CONTACT NETWORK

Write the names of people from your life—this is the beginning of your network!

Community or Volunteer Organizations	Religious Organizations	Sports Teams

Personal Business (Banker, Lawyer, Doctor, Dentist)	Hobbies/Clubs	Other Connections

NETWORKING

HOW TO APPROACH NETWORK MEETINGS

- Ask for a 30-minute face-to-face meeting and respect this time

- Use your professional objective and positioning statements

- Describe your marketing plan and provide a list of your target companies

- Provide your resume (hardcopy and follow up with a digital copy)

- Ask for their perspective regarding your target list—would they suggest adding or removing any target companies? Do they have any connections within these organizations?

- Offer useful information or assistance to your connection—make it a two-way street.

- Follow up with a thank you and other information they may be interested in after your meeting. This can be an email or a handwritten note.

- Keep them updated on your progress, especially with any of the connections they may have provided to you.

NETWORKING

LinkedIn TIPS FOR YOUR JOB SEARCH

LinkedIn is a job-seeker's best friend! This massive database will be critical to take advantage of in your job search strategy.

LinkedIn states the following 10 tips for networking on their database

1. 100% Complete Profiles = 40x More Opportunities

   Building connections starts with people seeing all you have to offer. LinkedIn will let you know how complete your profile is and will prompt you to fill in the blanks.

2. You're More Experienced Than You Think

   Think broadly about all your experience, including volunteer work, personal and professional organizations. You never know what might catch someone's attention.

3. Use Your Inbox

   Networking does not mean reaching out cold to strangers. Start building your LinkedIn network by uploading your online address book from your email account and connecting to people you know and trust.

4. Get Personal

   As you build your connections, customize your requests with a friendly note and if necessary, a reminder of where you met, whom you met through, or what organization you have in common.

5. Join the "In" Crowd

   LinkedIn Groups can help you form new connections. Start with your alumni groups and find volunteer organizations and associations you could join.

NETWORKING

LinkedIn TIPS FOR YOUR JOB SEARCH

6. **Lend a Virtual Hand**

   As you build connections, think about how you can support others. Comment on an individual's status update or forward a job listing to a friend—your generosity will be appreciated and returned.

7. **Update Your Status Early and Often**

   Stay on your network's radar by updating your LinkedIn status regularly—what you're reading, working on, and more.

8. **Request Informational Interviews**

   As a person entering the job market, don't ask professional contacts for a job. Instead, ask for a brief phone conversation to seek their job search advice. Alumni, family friends and industry leaders are often willing to help.

9. **Do Your Homework**

   Before an informational interview, a formal interview, or a networking event, use LinkedIn's advanced search and company pages to learn about the background and interests of the people you will be meeting.

10. **Step Away from the Computer**

    Support your online networking with a real human touch. Set up calls, attend live events, and mail old fashioned notes to people you interact with on LinkedIn.

NETWORKING

TYPES OF RECRUITERS

INTERNAL RECRUITERS—work solely for the company that employs them and understand the company and the players well. In most cases, these recruiters will have access to all open positions within their company and have strong relationships with the hiring managers. Internal recruiters are part of a talent acquisition team and are considered to be part of the human resource department.

CONTINGENCY SEARCH FIRM RECRUITERS—independent search firms with multiple clients. The contingency search firm receives payment if they place an individual within a company their client represents. These recruiters work with multiple clients and in most cases will not have as much insight as an internal recruiter. Companies often hire contingency recruiters to recruit for hard-to-fill positions or if the company does not have internal recruiting capabilities.

TEMPORARY STAFFING RECRUITERS—hire for temporary or contract positions within companies. These positions may lead to full-time jobs and can be a good way to "test" out a company and/or position.

RETAINED SEARCH FIRM RECRUITERS—companies pay retained search firms up front to conduct a search for key leaders in an organization. These tend to be executive level positions and the search process can be lengthy and costly.

All recruiters work on behalf of the employer, not the job-seeker. They review applications from job postings, but more often directly recruit qualified people who are currently employed and may not be actively looking for a new job opportunity.

NETWORKING

10 THINGS TO KNOW ABOUT WORKING WITH RECRUITERS

1. Treat every conversation as if you were on an actual job interview. Recruiters will determine if you are qualified to move into the interview process.

2. Building relationships with recruiters is very advantageous, as they have visibility into many opportunities within your target market.

3. Connect with recruiters via LinkedIn, as you will gain access to their connections. Many of these connections will be hiring managers.

4. Do your research prior to having a discussion with a recruiter. Recruiters have a reputation to uphold and will refer individuals who are qualified, motivated and are well-informed about the company and opportunity.

5. Make it easy for recruiters to find you via social media. Do not bombard them, but do connect with recruiters by sending messages to follow up on conversations and applications.

6. Provide recruiters with leads if appropriate, and other information they may find helpful. Recruiters remember good talent and will reach out as opportunities arise.

7. Recruiters are working with many people, resumes, and profiles at the same time. Things can slip through the cracks. Do not assume you are not qualified for a position simply because you did not hear back from a recruiter. Reach out with an open-ended question, such as, "Do you believe my background may be a good match for the Director of Human Resources position with XXX company?"

8. When possible, use a referral name when reaching out to a recruiter. Recruiters are much more likely to get back to you if you have been referred by an internal employee or someone they are familiar with—this is when your network comes into play.

9. Start with the highest level executive you know. If a recruiter receives a message from an executive in the company, even if it is a simple email being forwarded, they will follow up.

10. Express gratitude to recruiters, as they have the ability to get you in the door and through the process. Trust and honesty go a long way, just as in other relationships.

NETWORKING

6 TIPS WHEN COMMUNICATING WITH HIRING MANAGERS

1. Hiring managers make the final hiring decision, therefore these conversations are the most important in your job search.

2. Connecting with hiring managers prior to an actual hiring need can be extremely beneficial. If you have established a contact with a hiring manager before an actual opening, the communication is more conversational, and you may be able to circumvent a complex hiring process completely. It is expensive and time intensive for a hiring manager to interview applicants. If they have already identified talent in their network, they may never post the position.

3. Understand the pain points for the hiring manager and be prepared to show how you will add value to his/her team. Hiring managers will have the greatest sense of urgency to fill the roles on their team, therefore it is important to show your enthusiasm.

4. Hiring managers will rely on the opinion of the recruiter and other members of the interview panel. Make sure you are consistent with your message, focus on the needs of the hiring manager and link your benefits to their needs.

5. Understand that a hiring manager is looking for the best fit for the organization, as well as the most qualified person. It is helpful to know the company and department culture, as many hiring managers consider this the most important quality when making a hiring decision.

6. Hiring managers know all about you before you walk in the door. Most likely, hiring managers and/or the recruiter have researched not only your LinkedIn profile, but also your Facebook page and other social media sites. Be prepared for questions regarding anything they may uncover through an internet search.

REVIVING CAREERS

JOB SEARCH CAMPAIGNING

PHASE FOUR

CAMPAIGN

JOB SEARCH CAMPAIGNS

A well-constructed job search campaign is key to ensuring that you focus on priority actions and avoid wasting time and energy on unproductive activities. As with any project, a good plan helps you organize and prioritize your work and keeps you highly productive.

The goal of a job search campaign is to create awareness and build relationships in the industry where you would like to work.

Three steps for creating a job search campaign

STEP 1: CREATE YOUR STRATEGY

Define your smart goals — specific, measurable, attainable, relevant and time bound.

STEP 2: CREATE OBJECTIVES

After defining your goal, create measurable job search objectives. Your objectives will serve as the steps you take during your job search.

STEP 3: CHOOSE YOUR TACTICS

Once you have your goal and objectives in place, create tactics to implement your strategy. These tactics will be the driving force behind the promotion of your job search in order to get noticed by employers.

CAMPAIGN

JOB SEARCH CAMPAIGNS

Strategy Goals

Smart Goals—Specific, Measurable, Attainable, Relevant & Time Bound

SMART GOAL	TACTICS TO ACHIEVE GOAL	COMPLETION DATE			
Example: 5 In-Person Interviews	LinkedIn Messages Job Applications Emails to network	January 1st			

CAMPAIGN

CREATE OBJECTIVES AND CHOOSE TACTICS

CATEGORY	AVERAGE PER WEEK GOAL	AVERAGE PER WEEK ACTUAL
Total Hours on Job Search		
LinkedIn Messages		
LinkedIn Connections		
Job Applications		
Emails to Contacts		
Follow Up with Job Applications		
Face to Face Network Meetings		
Networking Events		
Join Professional Organizations		
Facebook Updates / Messages		

TOTAL LENGTH OF SEARCH: _____ WEEKS

CAMPAIGN

TARGET JOB AND COMPANIES WORKSHEET

What Do You Want to Do?	Where Do You Want to Do It?
Jobs that might be a fit	Companies to target

CAMPAIGN

TARGET MARKETS AND COMPANIES

Your target market is the group of organizations you plan to pursue. Your target market must be large, but manageable. We recommend starting with a target list of 30 companies. Your list will improve, change and refine as you weed out less desirable targets and add new targets through your networking efforts.

STEP 1—GATHER MARKETPLACE INFORMATION

Things to consider when choosing your targets:

- Industry
- Size
- Location
- Culture

STEP 2—GET YOUR MESSAGE OUT

Once you have established your initial target list and identified your contacts within these organizations, it is time to start reaching out.

Pursue Your Top Targets Each Week

- ❏ Set a goal of researching and connecting with 5-10 target companies per week
- ❏ Add 5 new organizations to your target list each week
- ❏ Re-prioritize your target list as you gather more information

CAMPAIGN

TARGET COMPANIES – SPREADSHEET SAMPLE

COMPANY	DESIRED POSITION Posted or Not Posted	CONTACTS WITHIN THE COMPANY	ACTION TO BE TAKEN	DATE CONNECTED

CAMPAIGN

TARGET COMPANIES – SPREADSHEET SAMPLE

COMPANY	DESIRED POSITION Posted or Not Posted	CONTACTS WITHIN THE COMPANY	ACTION TO BE TAKEN	DATE CONNECTED

CAMPAIGN

SEARCH METHODS

A job search is a marathon, not a sprint. No matter how qualified and talented you are, a job search takes time.

JOB SEARCH TACTICS THAT NO LONGER WORK

- Resume Blast Services
- Using the same resume for every job you apply for
- Completing online job applications and sitting back to wait for a reply

NEW JOB SEARCH TACTICS WITH A TARGETED APPROACH

- Think about your ideal job and write your summary paragraph explaining why you are perfect for that job. You should have many versions of this paragraph.
- Use networking methods vs. filling out another online job application.
- Discuss fulfilling the company's needs vs. talking about yourself. In your cover letter or your interview, focus on how you can eliminate the pain the hiring manager is feeling with the skills you can bring to the table.
- Think of yourself as a consultant, rather than a job-seeker.
- Have professional business cards printed immediately and start distributing them to your network.
- Be creative—send articles to the hiring managers. For example, "I thought you might be interested in this…" Make sure it will be helpful to them in their job.

CAMPAIGN

10 BEST SOURCES OF JOBS

1. **NETWORKING**
You are five times more likely to be hired if you have been referred than if you apply without knowing anyone associated with the company. Many companies have employee referral programs, which offer financial incentives if their referral is hired.

2. **EMPLOYER WEBSITE**
Look for a link to "current jobs" on the home page. While you are on the website, you may be able to sign up to have new jobs sent to you. Take note of the recruiter or hiring managers name associated with the job posting and connect with them on LinkedIn. If you apply to the position, also send a message to the individual to let them know you have applied and will be following up.

3. **LinkedIn**
LinkedIn is currently the most powerful and effective professional social network. LinkedIn has job postings (see the "jobs" link below the search bar at the top of every page) that you can apply to directly via the link. Also, look at the jobs tab in LinkedIn groups (you can join up to 100) and the company profile pages for your target employers. Use the "company page follow" to stay up to date with the company's activities and current events.

4. **JOB AGGREGATORS**
A job aggregator is a site that collects jobs postings from all around the world. These jobs are collected from employer websites, job boards, association websites, publications and more. You can upload your resume and list your job interests and these aggregators will push appropriate job openings to your email. The most powerful job aggregators today are Indeed.com, Monster.com and LinkUp.com

5. **SOCIAL MEDIA**
In addition to LinkedIn, job postings are available through both Twitter and Facebook. On Twitter, follow your target employers' Twitter accounts for news and look for a Twitter account for job opportunities. Many employers also have Facebook pages for both marketing and recruiting.

CAMPAIGN

10 BEST SOURCES OF JOBS

6. JOB BOARDS

Job Boards are not as popular as they once were, although it is worth checking the Niche Job Boards for your industry. Job boards can be found through your Internet search engine.

7. RECRUITERS AND STAFFING FIRMS

Recruiters can help you or hurt you. The important thing to remember is that they don't work for you, they work for the employer. Recruiters are in the position to screen you in or out, prior to any interaction with the company.

8. CLASSIFIED ADS IN PUBLICATIONS

Employers can use low cost or free sites in many locations. This low cost attracts small employers who can't easily post jobs on their own website. Do be cautious, as scams can be posted here.

9. ASSOCIATIONS AND ALUMNI GROUPS

Associations and school alumni groups are very effective for networking and often their websites have job postings for members. You can also connect with these associations and alumni groups through LinkedIn.

10. GOOGLE

Google has excellent tools for finding job postings, although this is not used as frequently.

CAMPAIGN

FINDING JOBS ONLINE TODAY

Networking with others will be the most successful method of conducting your job search, although online job search strategy is still important. Changes in technology have impacted the way recruiters recruit. Changes in recruiting dramatically change effective job search strategies. Recruiters may never see your resume if the company's software screens your resume out.

➢ Employers and recruiters search the internet to learn more about you before seriously considering you for a job or inviting you to an interview. If they can't find you, you are usually not considered for their jobs. Be "find-able" online.

➢ Recruiters will find you when they search online for qualified candidates. "Sourcing" is an employer's favorite way to fill jobs and is the quickest way to identify quality candidates. Have your LinkedIn profile updated and be visible on job board sites, such as Monster and Indeed. Google yourself to ensure your social media sites are clean and appropriate.

➢ Recruiters will be able to verify the facts on your resume or application and get a sense of your "fit" with their organization. Without appropriate online visibility, you are effectively invisible. Recruiters and employers are generally suspicious of invisible people, assuming it is because the person is not technologically up-to-date or has something to hide.

To avoid wasting valuable time and energy searching for job postings, do not apply for a job unless you are qualified—don't be a "resume spammer."

*We recommend you spend one-third of your available job search time and energy applying for, responding to, and following up on job ads, one-third reaching out to target employers you have identified on your own (whether they have posted job ads or not) and one-third of your time and energy networking.

*Remember that not every employer is right for you. You are interviewing the company as carefully as they are interviewing you. The goal is to find the ideal match.

INTERVIEWING AND JOB OFFERS

PHASE FIVE

INTERVIEWING

TYPES OF INTERVIEWS

SCREENING INTERVIEW

This is typically a phone call with the recruiter/gatekeeper, to verify the facts on your resume and to get a "feel" via your communication style if you may be a potential fit with the company/department. Screening interviews are generally conducted over the phone and scheduled for 15-30 minutes.

➤ Be clear, listen carefully to the questions and be concise with your answers

➤ Make sure you are consistent with your resume facts

➤ Show enthusiasm in your voice

➤ Ask to come onsite to meet with the recruiter or hiring manager

TELEPHONE INTERVIEW

Many hiring managers choose to conduct the first interview over the phone. These interviews can be tough to interpret as you do not have the benefit of body language. The best part of a phone interview is that you have the gift of invisibility, so use this to your advantage.

❏ Have your notes, resume, extensive bullet points about your skills and experience and a full list of questions written out in front of you

❏ Dress up to help you achieve the right professional mindset

❏ Use a land line phone or make sure your mobile is charged and will not lose reception

❏ Choose a quiet environment with no distractions

❏ Wait a half-second before starting to answer any question to make sure the interviewer is finished speaking. This technique is important when you cannot see body language, and cell phones may have a slight delay.

❏ Slow down your speaking pace, as phones can intensify the pace of your words

❏ After the interview, thank the interviewer and ask for the next steps

❏ If you are not offered a next step, ask if there are any concerns about you or your background in regard to being a fit for the position. This will allow you to address the concerns of being screened out and it shows initiative.

> ** If the call concludes without a commitment for a next step, you will most likely not be invited for an onsite interview.*

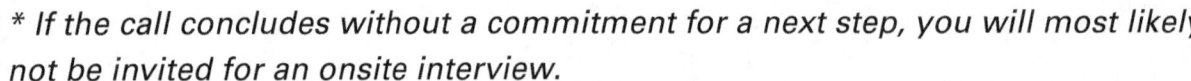

INTERVIEWING

TYPES OF INTERVIEWS

TRADITIONAL INTERVIEW

In this instance, an individual interviewer will ask you a series of questions designed to help him/her determine if you are a strong candidate for the job. These will vary in style, as some are professional interviewers and others may only interview someone once a year. Behavioral-based interview questions (described on page 63) may be asked or the "old-school" approach may still be used. The key is to follow the interviewer's lead.

- Use a firm, although not bone-crushing, handshake
- Make eye contact to convey trust and confidence during an interview
- Make the interviewer feel comfortable—people hire people they like and those who have the ability to engage in pleasant conversation
- Listen carefully, answer the questions honestly and do not be shy about your accomplishments

PANEL INTERVIEW

Panel interviews have several different formats. The most common is back-to-back 30-minute interviews with approximately 3-8 different individuals over the course of a day. These can be overwhelming at times but will give you insight into many divisions of the organization. Another panel format is having a group of interviewers in the same room, each taking turns to ask a question. In a group interview, determine who is asking the question, as each interviewer will consider your responses differently. Answer the question directly, but then elaborate further by adding points to address the perspectives of the other interviewers.

The panel will conduct a debrief meeting privately after your interview to discuss your strengths, concerns and next steps. The hiring manager will make the final decision, but will take the opinion of the panel members seriously.

- Understand who you are meeting with—titles, responsibilities and backgrounds
- Be consistent with your positioning statement throughout all interviews
- Have 2-3 different questions prepared for each interviewer
- Take interest in each panel member and learn how you could make a positive impact on the productivity for their specific function

INTERVIEWING

TYPES OF INTERVIEWS

TECHNICAL INTERVIEW

Technical interviews are used to assess your skills onsite. This is most often used for positions requiring hands-on expertise, such as a programming, writing or engineering. Basically, your interviewers want to see that you are capable of performing the necessary components of the job rather than simply trusting your resume.

- Understand and clarify what you will be asked to do and be prepared
- Ask questions if needed
- Have energy, stay positive, calm and be confident
- If working with a team, lead but do not overpower

VIDEO/SKYPE INTERVIEW

Video interviews are conducted when the hiring manager or the panel members interview you from a remote location. These can be individual interviews or panel interviews. You will need a computer with a camera and a Skype account. Conduct a test Skype call with a friend to ensure that there are no technical difficulties.

- Find a quiet, clean environment and make sure your mic is turned on
- Dress professionally, yes—the interviewers can see you!
- Create a digital chemistry using slow, confident, professional language
- Focus your eyes on the camera, not the view of the screen (eye contact)

INTERVIEWING

COMPANY RESEARCH

WHY RESEARCH COMPANIES?

It is important to have up-to-date and in-depth knowledge of a company, to allow you to engage in an educated conversation with key decision makers. You will ask well-thought-out questions and show you can add value to the organization if you truly understand the challenges they may be facing. Understanding a company and how they are positioned in the marketplace will allow you to make better decisions. Make sure you tailor your answers to the specific needs of the company.

WHAT SHOULD I DO?

- ❏ Look at the company websites
- ❏ Understand the competitors in the market place
- ❏ Know the company's mission statement and values
- ❏ Understand the company size, locations and history
- ❏ Review the financial health of the company by listening to the quarterly earning conference calls and by reviewing the company annual report
- ❏ Take note of the current stock price and market share
- ❏ Look at the profile of the key executives of the company and the individuals you may meet during your interview process. (What companies did they work for? Where did they attend school? What are their personal interests?) This information can be found on LinkedIn, Facebook and the company website
- ❏ Read a variety of newspapers (local and world news), industry magazines, trade journals and blogs, not simply before an interview, but on a daily basis to stay educated and informed
- ❏ Follow your target companies on LinkedIn, Facebook and Twitter

INTERVIEWING

SECURING THE INTERVIEW

The interview is the single most important step in getting a job and is the culmination of all your networking efforts. The interview is your opportunity to market and sell yourself by demonstrating what your skills, experience and qualifications can do for the company.

Smart ways to secure an interview today

USE THE BACKDOOR

Once you know the job title and location, research on LinkedIn or Google to find the name of the hiring manager or department head. If you cannot find a name, call and ask the receptionist for the name of department manager. Use the job posting as a lead to work rather than an application button to press.

GET AN EMPLOYEE REFERRAL

Having a current employee at the company refer you is the best way to get an interview. Even better if this referral will give you a personal recommendation.

BE DIFFERENT

Companies are looking for people who can think "outside the box" and may grant interviews based on innovation alone.

CHECK JOB POSTINGS FOR SIMILAR JOBS

If the company is hiring for similar jobs, make sure you know who is handling all the requisitions. You can easily be overlooked if you apply directly to only one position.

USE HIGHER AUTHORITY

In your email message, let the recipient know you are also sending your resume to others within the company, such as the hiring manager or another senior executive. People will be reluctant to ignore your request if you are a qualified applicant and the people you also contact are more senior.

INTERVIEWING

SECURING THE INTERVIEW

BECOME A PASSIVE CANDIDATE

Right or wrong, passive candidates are more desirable than active candidates. In your email, mention that an associate sent you a link to the job description and since you're not actively looking, you would like to learn more before you become a serious candidate. You will still need to prove you are a viable prospect but being harder to get makes you more desirable.

CUSTOMIZE YOUR EMAILS

Do not send generic template emails. Customize your message to the individual and ask for a response.

REDUCE THEIR RISK

There will be a perceived risk in hiring someone who is new to the workforce, especially if you're not a perfect match. One way to minimize the company's risk is to offer to work on a contract or consulting basis until you can prove you're capable of handling the job. Just offering this option can change how you are perceived as a candidate.

TAKE SMALL STEPS

It is much easier to arrange an exploratory phone conversation with a hiring manager than arrange a formal onsite interview. In most cases, this is the first step in the formal interview process and should be considered extremely important.

INTERVIEWING

10 STEPS IN PREPARING FOR AN INTERVIEW

1. Conduct in-depth research on the company, industry and competitors so you understand the organization's reputation in the marketplace.

2. Have a solid reason for why you would like to work for the company.

3. Research all interviewers and take notes on their current role and responsibilities. Review interviewers past companies, education and interests. The interviewer will be impressed you spent the time to understand their background and it will help break the ice.

4. Prepare a variety of specific questions for each interviewer based on their role within the company. Each person will have a different view on the company culture and the perceived priorities of the open position.

5. Be prepared to answer behavior-based interview questions with specific examples of past accomplishments and practice out loud/ role play.

6. If you have any contacts within the company, reach out to let them know you will be onsite to interview and ask them to give you a positive referral.

7. Plan to dress professionally, unless the interviewer specially requests you dress casually. Appearance is important!

8. Be organized and have multiple copies of your resume on hand. Map out the company location prior to the interview and plan to arrive 10-15 minutes early.

9. Be confident in your positioning statement, focusing on what you know the employer needs. Be ready to expand upon and tailor your positioning statement to match the needs of the organization.

10. Relax, turn your cell phone off, and enjoy the process. Have a goal in mind to achieve by the end of the interview, such as moving to the next step in the process.

INTERVIEWING

10 TIPS FOR INTERVIEW DAY

Interviewers form immediate judgments about applicants—usually in the first 30-60 seconds of a meeting. Make your first impression count!

1. Arrive 10-15 minutes early—never be late to an interview.

2. Be positive and courteous to everyone you meet—strike up a conversation with the receptionist. She will let the recruiter know how nice you are.

3. Be professional and do not share personal information such as marital status, children or your age when asked to introduce yourself. Use your positioning statement and remain consistent throughout your interviews.

4. Listen well—do not dominate the interview. Answer the question asked; don't go off on tangents. Listen carefully to what is being asked and clarify the question if necessary.

5. Be relaxed, confident and humble—these are the three most important intangible signs interviewers look for in a potential candidate.

6. Be honest and always respond to questions with a positive answer.

7. Do not discuss salary or benefits in a first interview unless the interviewer initiates the conversation.

8. Be respectful of the time allotment for the interview. Ask how much time the interviewer has to spend with you and use this time wisely.

9. Ask at least two intelligent, specific and insightful questions.

10. Learn interviewer's pain points and be ready to address how you will be able to help.

After the Interview, send a thank you email to all interviewers expressing your appreciation for their time, follow up on a specific topic you discussed and express your interest in the company.

INTERVIEWING

ASKING THE RIGHT QUESTIONS

Asking questions shows the interviewer that you genuinely care about the position, the company and the role should you be hired. Interviews should be a two-way street and the goal is to learn as much as you can about your potential employer through a dialogue interview approach.

* Do not ask for information that can be found on the organizations website, instead ask insightful questions that will allow you to get to know the culture, the company and the expectations for the role.

SAMPLE QUESTIONS TO ASK IN THE INTERVIEW

- In your opinion, what makes this organization a great place to work?
- What do you consider the most important criteria for success in this job?
- What are the company's short-term and long-term goals?
- What role will this position play in achieving these goals?
- Can you walk me through a typical day?
- I have reviewed the job description, and would appreciate your view on what the most important responsibilities of this role will be.
- What is the priority for this role, and how can I make an immediate impact?
- Can you please explain the reporting structure of the department?
- Tell me about the organization's culture.
- How would you describe the organization's management style?
- Why is this position open and are any internal candidates being considered for the role?
- Do you have any concerns about my background or the gap in my employment and how it relates to this role?
- I am very interested in the position. What are the next steps in the hiring process?

INTERVIEWING

QUESTIONS TO PREPARE FOR WHEN RE-ENTERING THE WORKFORCE

"TELL ME ABOUT YOURSELF"

Use your positioning statement, focusing on what you know the employer needs. The best way to respond to this question is to expand upon your positioning statement to match the needs of the company.

I am (profession/level) _____

With expertise in (functions or capabilities) _____

My strengths include (unique professional qualities) _____

For example, (explain accomplishments of distinction relative to the role) _____

I have worked with/for (types of organizations and industries) _____

"WHY DO YOU WANT TO RE-ENTER THE WORKFORCE NOW?"

What the interviewer will be listening for:

- ✓ How serious is she about re-entering the workforce?
- ✓ Does she know what position she wants and have the skills to excel in this capacity?
- ✓ Is she willing to work hard and put in the hours required?
- ✓ Is she interested in a long-term career?
- ✓ Will she fit into the company culture?
- ✓ Will she take direction (possibly from someone younger)?
- ✓ Is she confident, self-motivated and willing to ask questions?

INTERVIEWING

TRADITIONAL VS. BEHAVIORAL-BASED INTERVIEWS

Companies are becoming more strategic with behavioral-based interviewing. The premise behind behavioral interviewing is that the most accurate predictor of future performance is past performance in similar situations. Behavioral-based interviewing will probe more deeply, and your answers will be truer to your character.

Your responses need to be specific and detailed. Candidates who tell the interviewer about a specific situation that relates to each question will be far more effective and successful than those who respond in general terms (use those success stories from pages 20-21 — situation, action, outcome).

EXAMPLES OF TODAY'S BEHAVIOR BASED QUESTIONS

- Provide a specific example of a time when you used good judgment in solving a problem
- Discuss the types of leadership roles you have held in the past
- Please explain how you have used team building skills
- Give me an example of a time when you set a goal and achieved it
- Tell me about a time when you had to use your presentation skills to influence others
- Relate a specific example of a time when you had to conform to a policy with which you did not agree
- Give me an example of a time when your biggest weakness at work kept you from reaching a goal
- Describe your typical way of dealing with conflict and give me an example
- Tell me about a difficult professional decision you have made in the last year
- Provide an example of a time when you failed
- Tell me about a time when you were forced to make an unpopular decision

INTERVIEWING

CULTIVATING AND NEGOTIATING JOB OFFERS

After all the hard work you have done researching, applying and interviewing for jobs it is understandable that you will be excited when you are offered a position. Congratulate yourself, although do not be so quick to accept it right away.

When an employer makes a job offer, they are laying their cards on the table and giving up their power. The recruiter/hiring manager will want the candidate to accept the position right away. This is never a good idea for you, the candidate, as you want time to think and formulate your response.

WHAT TO DO ONCE A VERBAL OFFER HAS BEEN EXTENDED

- Thank the person who made the offer, while showing enthusiasm and appreciation.

- Request an official written offer. This should include the name of the position, a start date, a salary, your manager, and details of the company benefit package. The official letter will give you a chance to review the details thoroughly to ensure you completely understand the company's offer.

- Determine the date the company needs your final answer after receiving the letter. If the employer tells you they need an immediate answer, that is not a good sign. Pressuring is a scare tactic—most employers understand this is a big decision and most allow 1-2 days to consider the offer and respond.

- If you would like to negotiate the offer or clarify details, say "I have considered the offer and it is an excellent opportunity; I would like to discuss the offer in more detail, may we please set up a time to speak or meet?"

- When you are ready to accept the offer, reiterate all the details as you understand them. If any changes have been made through negotiations, ask for a revised offer letter to sign.

- Once you have verbally accepted the position, ask about the next steps. For example, you will need dates for on-boarding paperwork, orientation date, and drug screen testing. Ask the hiring manager how you can start preparing prior to your first day. This will demonstrate your proactive interest, reaffirming the recruiter's/hiring manager's choice to extend an offer.

INTERVIEWING

NEGOTIATING YOUR SALARY AND SETTING EXPECTATIONS

Employers expect negotiations at some point during the hiring process. Negotiating is a skill and if done effectively, will impress your potential manager. Feel confident when asking questions and remember, they extended the offer to you and want you to join their company.

10 QUESTIONS YOU MAY WANT TO ASK PRIOR TO ACCEPTING THE JOB OFFER

1. Is the job description you provided accurate?
2. What is the start date? If needed, is this flexible?
3. How and when will I be evaluated? Will there be a compensation increase based on this evaluation?
4. Will you please provide me with a copy of the benefits? When will I be eligible to receive them?
5. Is this a firm offer?
6. Is the salary negotiable?
7. Is this base only or total compensation? (This will open a discussion about bonuses and stock options)
8. Will I be eligible for stock options and/or do you have an employee stock purchase program?
9. Will there be a sign-on bonus?
10. What are the office work hours? Is there flexibility to work remotely? Are expenses, such as parking, reimbursed?

IMPORTANT TIPS

- Don't completely stop your job search or cut off other options until your first day on the job. Your employer will not stop recruiting until you start employment.
- If you receive an offer, do not be afraid to let other potential employers know this, as it can speed up the offer process with other companies. Timing can be tricky, but you want to make sure you have all offers on the table prior to your final employment decision.

TRANSITIONING INTO THE WORKFORCE

PHASE SIX

TRANSITION

TRANSITION INTO THE WORKPLACE

Your job search project has ended, but your career is just beginning. It is normal to feel anxious on your first day, but remember, the hiring manager has asked you to join them as they believe you are the right match for the organization.

Have a plan and use the checklist below on your first day of employment:

- ❏ Close the loop with any outstanding organizations you may still be interviewing with
- ❏ Notify your contacts of your new status and thank them for their support
- ❏ Inform all the recruiters you may have been working with of your new role
- ❏ Update your LinkedIn profile and confirm all your information is correct
- ❏ Update your Facebook status and make sure the content is clean
- ❏ Help prepare the announcement your company will use internally to introduce you
- ❏ Develop a list of topics to discuss with your new boss and ask how they prefer to communicate
- ❏ Set up a regular meeting and save your time-sensitive questions for this alloted time frame. Make sure to discuss your boss's priorities
- ❏ Create your operating calendar and organize your desktop
- ❏ Prepare a strategy to meet key individuals within the organization and begin developing strong relationships with them
- ❏ Disarm any individuals that may be threatened by your arrival through open communication
- ❏ Look for ways to support the needs of others early on
- ❏ Study organizational charts to understand hierarchy of departments
- ❏ Create a strategy for analyzing the readiness of the organization to accept any changes you plan to initiate
- ❏ Understand your need for professional development and enlist assistance
- ❏ Be observant of the "norms" of the organization/department. These are behaviors that have evolved over time, although will not be written down or verbalized.

It is normal to feel overwhelmed and tired during your first months of employment. Approach each day as a new day to contribute and learn. Be resourceful, proactive and willing to go above and beyond your written job description. You will soon be entrenched and a vital part of the organization!

TRANSITION

TECHNOLOGY IN THE WORKPLACE

Re-entry into the workforce can be challenging, as technology has radically changed in the past decade. In today's job market, it's not only IT job applicants who need technical skills. With technology constantly changing, employers everywhere are looking for tech-savvy job candidates for non-tech related positions. This means that administrative, creative, sales, marketing and other non-IT job seekers are required to have relatively strong backgrounds and skill sets to stay competitive.

There are basic technology skills you will want to be familiar with when you start your new position. Of course, roles will vary in their usage of technology.

To make your transition smoother, we recommend you become familiar with the following:

- ✓ Social media sites (Linkedin, Facebook, Instagram, Twitter)
- ✓ Microsoft Word
- ✓ Microsoft Excel
- ✓ Power Point
- ✓ Microsoft Office (email, calendar & meetings)
- ✓ Skype videoconferencing
- ✓ Conference calls
- ✓ Database management

TRANSITION

LONG TERM CAREER PLANNING

You will want to maintain your career momentum and continue to work towards goals that will allow you and your career to evolve and advance.

WHAT IS IMPORTANT?

- Continue to survey your professional environment
- Keep current on what is happening in your industry
- Continue to join networks and associations for your profession
- Understand how you fit into the ongoing plans of your organization
- Determine what you need to do to enhance your skills and competencies to achieve your next career goal
- Set a goal for your career advancement and manage your timeline
- Document your accomplishments and achievements on a weekly basis
- Keep your resume current
- Analyze your likes/dislikes and continue to evaluate your position
- Identify career and employment trends and understand how you can prepare for future changes and developments
- Establish a solid network of people and communicate on a regular basis
- Help and support others in your network
- Never burn a bridge!

A full career plan should have a long-term vision and mission. This is the future state you want your career to be and how you will achieve it. A series of short-term and medium-term objectives should serve as the stepping stones to this vision. Short-term goals (1-2 years), such as skills, experiences and accomplishments will help you reach the medium-term objectives. Medium-term goals (3-5 years) will place you on the correct path for your long-term vision.

Continue to identify your plateaus, succeed in reaching the plateau and find the next plateau. This will allow you to connect the dots between your current situation and your long-term career plan.

> "I've come to believe that each of us has a personal calling that's as unique as a fingerprint—and that the best way to succeed is to discover what you love and then find a way to offer it to others in the form of service, hard work, and also allowing the energy of the universe to lead you." —Oprah Winfrey

You are more powerful than you know!